T0128419

THIS I *SWEAR* IS TRUE

MARILYN MOORE

authorHOUSE®

AuthorHouse™
1663 Liberty Drive
Bloomington, IN 47403
www.authorhouse.com
Phone: 1 (800) 839-8640

Published by AuthorHouse 06/13/2019

ISBN: 978-1-7283-1524-9 (sc)
ISBN: 978-1-7283-1518-8 (e)

Library of Congress Control Number: 2019907529

Print information available on the last page.

Any people depicted in stock imagery provided by Getty Images are models, and such images are being used for illustrative purposes only. Certain stock imagery © Getty Images.

This book is printed on acid-free paper.

This book goes to my CREATOR GOD, MY FATHER, AND BLESSED MOTHER, THEY WERE ALWAYS WITH ME.

And it shall come to pass that everyone who calls upon the name of the Lord shall be saved.

Acts 2:21 (ESV)

'YOU HAVE CANCER!" "YOU HAVE CANCER!" Right then a Doctor put his hands on me, My Shoulder's turns me toward him, He stood in front of me and kept saying "LOOK AT ME!" "YOUR CANCER HAS SPREAD!". "YOUR IN DENIAL!" "YOU NEED THE TREATMENTS!" "YOU HAVE A FEW MONTHS TO LIVE!" "YOU NEED CHEMO AND RADIATION!" "IT IS GOING TO SPREAD TO YOUR LUNGS, AND YOUR BRAIN!" I TOLD THEM "JUST TAKE THE BREASTS OUT." DOCTOR SAID, "YOUR TOO FAR GONE". I said no to the treatments, Doctor then told me I needed to make my directives. I took a good best friend with me, she was an attorney, Nancy Reyes she just jumped right up from her seat and started yelling at the doctor. "WHAT ARE YOU TELLING HER?" "SHE IS DYING?" "WHAT IS HAPPENING?" I felt my mind like "WHERE AM I?" "AM I CRAZY?" "I AM DYING?" "CANCER?" "THIS IS A DREAM" "A FEW MONTHS?" "THIS IS WHAT IT FEELS LIKE?' "CANCER" "I DON'T LOOK LIKE I DO NOT FEEL LIKE I AM DYING. "NOW WHAT?"

"HOW AM I SUPPOSED TO ACT?" "HOW AM I GOING TO TELL MY CHILDREN?" "I WANNA LAUGH." Then you think "NO! NO! NO! "THIS IS ALL."

"SO, THIS IS THE END?

THIS IS JUST THE BEGINNING

My father always said he was going to live till he was 99.9 years old. He died March, 1999. He was 71yrs old, he died of Cirrhosis of the liver. He was sick for a few years, and it got worse toward the end, you could see in his eyes he was dying, they get with their eyes glazed and hold the sheets like they are covering themselves, holding tightly. Wide eyed, my dad asked me "Marilyn, Am I going to Hell?" He was scared I could see that. I asked him "Dad, your 71 years old. Have you ever seen Devil?' He said "No", I then told him there is no burning Hell, no devil, but dad, you will pay for all the things you have done". He was stunned, and said "How do you know this?" I said I don't know, but it is just coming out of my mouth. "But a Hell, no hell." I saw him lean back and drew a deep breath, and relaxed with a nice smile on his face. He died. Before I left, I whispered in his ear, "Have a great journey. I kissed Him, I said "I love you"." You know Dad in all my life you never told me you loved me."

With that I left.

I did dream of him a couple of days later, he was calling me from this hill, standing next to my Mom who raised me, he looked so young, healthy and happy.

He was calling me, "Marilyn,!' 'Marilyn,!' I want to let you know I am okay," I am asking her for forgiveness. "but I am okay" I told him "Dad, you look nice". He looked nice, handsome and well. I was so happy and yes, it was so nice, he was happy. I did tell my brother's, they just shook heads. My brothers were at my house and we sitting around the table, talking about the arrangements, for My father. 20 Years ago we only had answering machine, I saw a message, I told my family "Oh maybe Someone is calling about the services, well, I checked out, AMAZING AS TO WHAT I HEARD!! IN A VERY RASPY TONE "I LOVE YOU", "BOY OH BOY" SHOCKED FACES!' Number was unknown, I let everyone listen they were so amazed. My son wanted to record it, he tried and tried, but would not record. it lasted 31 days. IT WAS MY DAD, they all knew it, it was his raspy old voice. I do believe in AFTER LIFE AWARENESS, coincidence, THERE ARE NO COINCIDENCES IN LIFE. To this day they talk about it. I have had many encounters from people who have passed in my life. Dreams, or just knowing they around. Songs are the best or if they remind me of something funny. It is so wonderful to know.

First time, after my Grandfather passed, I was pregnant with my son, I dreamt of my Grandfather, he Got me and hugged me said I was beautiful. I was going through some hard times, my husband was Cheating, problems in the marriage. I feel they come around to comfort.

My Father in law passed, I was attending services, but with his 3 grandchildren, which he truly loved, we sat in the back, like way in the back, no one acknowledged the grandkids. I was just going thru the divorce, I never told anyone my problems and my mother-in law did and could not see it. She was upset with me. I went home and I decided not to attend the church the following day. I woke up in the morning, with this nagging voice. "Go!! Go he loved your kids. So, I get up and I hurried Got the kids dressed, knowing I was going to be late, when I was on the way I told Grandpa Charlie," I am late and the cars are probably all lined up and I am going to be the last car. I was feeling bad because of his grandchildren, and how they were ignored. So, I finally arrive and yes, all the cars were lined up, just like I knew, first the Hearse then I saw the limousine and but to my surprise, gosh! low and behold right in back of the limo was a empty parking space! I said, YES! THANK YOU GRAMPA CHARLIE! I PUT HANDS UP! HE HONORED US! At the end of the line, last car was my Husband!!

Remembering my wonderful grandmother, she was my wonderful person who help me thru everything. When she was passing, I was at the hospital because my daughter was having her first baby. I was going to be a grandmother, but I had to tell my daughter, I was sorry I could not stay, but I had to leave because they called to tell me that my grandmother was passing, when I got there, I was so upset they had her with no gown and uncovered, I told them to cover her and they said she did not know I told them they were nuts, cover her. I told them to just keep her with no pain, and they had the heart monitor on her, I was thanking her for all her wonderful years with me, I told her how I loved her. Tears were coming out of her eyes, I knew she was crying she had not seen my father, her favorite son in 2 years, I went out looking for him at 1 am to find him, I left messages at all the bars let him know his mother was passing. I went back to the hospital and I told my grandmother that I did not find him, tears came down her eyes, the priest came in to give her the sacrament of LAST RITES. When he finished, the heart monitor went on flat lined, I was so sad, I was saying to myself Goodbye My grandma bye, bye and I saw a beautiful white light leaving her body. I was just to beautiful and just going up like a wave swirling. I was so amazed, I HAD READ ON THIS BUT I NEVER FIGURED. My uncle, my brothers, my aunt was there also, around 3am. Then all of sudden miraculously the heart monitor started Up again, everyone startled and we look at the door entrance it was my dad, I told him DAD! SHE CAME BACK SHE SAW YOU! TALK TO HER, I ushered everyone out, so my dad could talk with her, he was Crying, telling her "MOM," PLEASE DON'T DIE, I WILL TAKE CARE OF YOU HE JUST CRIED, AND SHE PASSED.

A few years had passed and we were with the family and I was telling my uncle and aunt that I am pretty sane person, but I saw something when grandma died, I know it was not my imagination. All of a sudden 3 of them stood up and said "YOU SAW THE WHITE LIGHT LEAVING HER BODY!" I said "YES", they did too but did not say anything, WOW! OH WOW! AGAIN "NO COINCIDENCE! These are just a few of my family members stories that passed, that I am sharing, I have had some other stories of other family members, almost all who have passed.

I was taken to church by my great aunt at 3 years of age, she always wore a black dress and veil, she was so nice to me tiny woman. The church was so beautiful. My biological mother had four children from father. They were not together I remember him coming to visit. One day he came and gave a quarter, I put it in my mouth and was choking on it.

My great Aunt was the first to take me to church. I was 3 years old, and she took me to this big beautiful church, I was in total awe. We went inside, it was so wonderful to see and felt so good. I was standing in front of this statue of a beautiful lady, it was Jesus Mother Mary. I couldn't take my eyes off her. My mother was in the General Hospital having a surgery on her Thyroid.

The Hospital made a mistake with her surgery and they destroyed her vocal cords. My great aunt told me "Pray for your mom. She will make her well. I did. My mother's recovery time was going to be a long time. My brothers and I were separated going to different places.

I went to live with my Dad's parents and my brothers, went to different family members. I loved living with my grandparents, it was a wonderful, wonderful life, like "FATHER KNOWS BEST" "OZZIE AND HARRIET", ALSO "DONNA REED".

I was taught to say prayers, every night my grandmother would listen to me, she would comb my hair, Take me to school, told me not to talk to strangers or go with anyone, just her. I always felt so special with her. She had this certain perfume she used "TABOO" always wore. I loved it.

When both grandparents took me to church, they were so involved with the Church. "OUR LADY OF LOURDES". Back in 1949, my grandfather donated the land to have the school built. A movie was made about "St Bernadette" I would watch it over and over again. I loved the school, just being there. I was just really lucky to have been able to attend. It was just true fate.

My mother was still recovering from her illness. My father remarried, a very beautiful, classy nice woman. She had no children of her own, she had been in a hospital when she was 14 years old, till 30 years, there was an epidemic of Turberculosis, they removed a lung from her and she was well. They took us happily to live with them. I remember her pet peeve not to be called "Stepmom", that was A NO NO. I can truly say she was such a great teacher of life. She had no children, she was around 32 yrs of age She was very generous, a great listener. My dad did not appreciate her as the years went on. One time they argued and she left. I was like 6 years old, I cried so much. She came back. I truly loved her. We attended Our Lady of Lourdes school, I remember seeing Jesus Mother when I first entered my room, I would just come in and look at it, I loved the story, I heard it over and over, my children heard it, my grandchildren did also.

I learned about religion, when I was in the first grade, I would pray at night and I would have my hands up and tell "JESUS SHOW ME YOUR FACE. PLEASE, PLEASE, I WON'T TELL!" All the time I would ask this. I always negotiated with Jesus, during that time I heard of bad things on the news happening to little girls, so I asked him almost every year to let me live one more year. I truly believed. My brother asked me if I remembered, when we were in grammar school, I would not let them leave to school, before I blessed them and I would make them kiss Mother Mary's picture. I did not remember. I prayed so hard when my grandmother had an operation, I was so scared, I promised Jesus that I would become a Nun if he made my grandma well. He made her well. I did not keep that promise. I am sorry. My Children attended Lourdes, and so did my grandchildren, so as you can see, we as our family is so Connected to OUR LADY OF LOURDES. I truly taught them all about the story of St. Bernadette over and over. We lived across the street, to OUR LADY OF LOURDES CHURCH AND SCHOOL. My grandparents made the visit to FRANCE, to the healing waters.

We all graduated from high school. My brothers join the service, it was in 1969 the "Viet Nam Era. Before my brother went he wanted his blessing and I gave my brother a picture of St. Joseph with the baby Jesus, I told him to always keep it on him, lovely prayer, it stated that whoever had possession, whoever read it, would never die in the hands of the enemy, or in a fire or sudden death.

He took it and Yes, he was in the jungles of Viet Nam. One day I get this call, a Frantic call at around 3 AM, my brother, "MARILYN! "MARILYN! PLEASE, PLEASE I NEED MORE OF THOSE PRAYERS, SEND ME A LOT OF THEM! THIS MORNING IN THE BARRACKS SOMEONE THREW A GRENADE, I TOOK OUT MY PRAYER AND BEGAN TO PRAY OUT LOUD THE GUYS WERE ALL IN BACK OF ME!" ROSALIE IT DID NOT GO OFF!! IT DID NOT GO OFF, EVERYONE IS IN SHOCK AND WANT THE PRAYER!! So yes, I got right on It and sent him the prayer, throughout his term I was mailing them out all the time.

To this day he still mails them to the ones over Sea's.

So, all my life I believed and I prayed. I had 3 children, when I was going to have my first baby, I asked God, and Mother Mary not to let me have pain, I want to have a baby like she had BABY JESUS, I even took her picture when it was time for me to deliver. I remember the girls in there Screaming "NURSE, NURSE HELP ME IT HURTS! I just kept her picture in my hands, well, I had my daughter in 3 hours, yes, I was surprised. Let me say this, after reviewing everything in my life now at this age, I get that things are all done for a purpose, again no coincidences, I truly see that. my Mom never had a baby. Oh, yes, she raised 4 children, we were very young in age. Well, after I had my daughter I had to stay in bed. I could not get up, so I stood with my mother. I was so weak, she put the bassinet in her room and for a whole month she stood home from work and she attended my baby, feedings all hours, bathing, diaper changes, and just attended to her Grandchild, she later asked me if she could baptize her and I said "ABSOLUTELY".

So, reflecting again GOD IS SO GREAT! I have come to the conclusion, that God gave my mom a baby, my daughter, to nurture and care for a new born, to bond and feel the love a new mother feels, and she got to do this. They became so close, my daughter were her eyes, she spoiled her, pampered, gave her anything she wanted.

I truly see that now, yes God is good.

All over the world, there have been apparitions of Mother Mary. She has asked for World Peace, and in France, the healing waters. In Mexico, there is Our Lady of Guadalupe, she appeared To this man and wanted a church built there, well he had told the church about it but, of course, they Need proof, Yes, he brought Roses to them, falling out of his cloak, it was very unusual to have Roses, at This time of the year, so it was fantastic. Juan Diego was his name he was so proud to take the Roses To the priests, he carried them in his poncho, when he let them come out, all the priest stood back, in Aww, was a picture of this beautiful Mother Mary, she imprinted on his Poncho. and they built a church there in her honor the cloak has been through a fire but was not burned.

The cloak was hung in the church and is still there. This was back in the 1600's.

To this day people make promises to her and she answers their prayers, and they go see her, in Mexico City. I made a promise to Our Lady of Guadalupe in Mexico, that if she gave me a boy, because back 70's we did not have MRI's I would go see her in Mexico. Yes, she gave me a beautiful baby boy. I gave her my thank you with so much praise and love promising I will go see her. Well, every year I would tell her, "This year I will go see you". Year after year went by, but I still promised.

One evening I went to the market and when I came home, there was a candle with her picture on it, I did not purchase. I told her ok I will go.

So, next day I put the television on and out pops up a series of her story. Wow! I went to the record Shop and out pops up a CD of her with songs. Well, I knew I just had to go she was telling me. I KNOW NOW THERE NO COINCIDENCES IN LIFE. It was NOW going to be 30 years, since the promise. Two weeks left I did make the trip, yes so wonderful. Yes, I was also shown she knew I was there! I went with a friend of mine and he even experience the beautiful sign, letting us know she knew I was there. So wonderful.

I always have prayed and negotiated. Lessons have been taught to me, thru prayer, great experiences, I Have 3 children, I got divorced, I was truly struggling, I was going to beauty school, I was around 30 Yrs Old. I did not have money for milk, driving to school I was praying and wondering where I would get it. During the day I cut and combed this woman's hair, she loved it and gave me $20.00 dollars, I thought thank you God,

Throughout my life he took care of me. I look back now, and many beautiful things have happened to me. He always took care of me, with birthdays, celebrations, a wedding, graduations, putting my son's threw school where they came out with their AA degree at the age of 19 years old. Yes, now looking back, I do not know how it was done. He never let us want.

Yes, I did teach my children that "GOD IS" and the wonderful things they have seen they just know.

All you have to do is "ASK".

The year is now 2006, December. I had this dream of my Father. I was sitting down in like an Auditorium. I saw a door opening on the side of a wall, and out marched this man, I look as He pivoted and started marching toward where I was sitting. It was my Dad, he marched right To me and knelt down close to me, I could see all his face, it was so wonderful to see him, I told Him "Dad it is so good to see you!" Amazing I could see the pores on his face. He looked at me and Put his head down and started to cry telling me "Marilyn! I have to tell you something". "I can't" "I just can't he got up and just marched back. He has a uniform on like a soldier. Well a month later, I I felt a lump on my breast, I goggled the symptoms, it was under the right breast. It did look like an Orange peel, wow! I could not believe it, but it was there. I was not working and I did not have insurance, but I went to this hospital White Memorial, Oscar de la Hoya, Clinic.

I told them I did not have money, but I had a tumor, they scheduled me for a mammogram right away, they did not even ask me anything.

As you know Oscar de la Hoya is a well know boxer, and this facility was because of his mother. She had died of breast Cancer. They found 2 tumors, and this was right around Christmas time. I was scheduled For a biopsy, and yes, Cancer was found. They wanted to remove both breasts, they said I would have Reconstruction, as big as I wanted. I told them just to take the tumors out, no reconstruction. They wanted to give me radiation, I refused. I know they were very upset with me. I scheduled the Surgery till after Christmas, I wanted to tell my children after, so I would not spoil Christmas, the Surgery was set for February the 4th.

I lived by myself, it was horrible, to know this and be by yourself. I was listening the radio late, late at Night. They were announcing how Switzerland were declaring" TUMERIC CURCUMIN A CANCER CURE" Upon the cancer cells commit suicide. I was thinking, tomorrow is going to be a great day! I never heard them talk about it. I did find it at a popular vitamin store. I started taking, this was around the beginning of the diagnosis.

I lived by myself, man, oh man did it leave me thinking. UGLY! UGLY! Stuff happening to me. I then remembered the dream of my dad. "YES"!! Now I know why my father could not tell me what I was going to go through. My poor, father. Yes, I cried, just thought about everything. But I kept strong till after Christmas.

New Year's Eve, I dreamt I was in the living room, and a man sat across from me and he was handsome, Nicely dressed, in a white shirt, nice slacks. He started to tell me how important family was, and All of a sudden I told him "Hey your JOHN KENNEDY JR!" He smiled and I woke up! I thought it was a Wonderful dream, I went to church, and the sermon was about "HOW IMPORTANT FAMILY IS".

Gee, how about that.

They changed the surgery to JAN 31,2007, I do not remember why, but, we were getting closer, I told my children and yes, they were very concerned, scared, and crying.

I did dream of all who had passed in my life, and I remember in the dream, I was so happy to see them Come and visit me. I was serving them coffee, and feeding them. Amazing!

I did dream of my grandmother, sitting in my bedroom, I saw her and said "Oh Grandma it is good to see You, she looked at me and said, "Marilyn, don't be like me, I always worried about everything! Don't be Like me everything is going to be fine." I love her, writing this right now, I so truly miss her.

This was in 2007, 2019 today "EVERYTHING IS FINE."

Surgery day is here. Set for 6:30 am. My children were there, my cousin jimmy, I was scared. On this day I was thinking about an aunt of mine, Isabel, she was always so nice to me. I was telling my Cousin Jimmy, and he just stood looking at me, he said, This is the anniversary of my Mother's death. I did not know. Isabel, died young, she had BREAST CANCER. I was in awe, I knew that I knew she was with me. They had changed the date from Feb. 4th to Jan 31 st. NO COINCIDENCE, IT WAS MEANT TO BE.

I did not have the surgery till 6:30 pm. When I was in the surgery room they had marked the MRI Hanging there I could see the tumors. The nurse was going round and round, the doctor said, "Nurse what is happening, she said, "Doctor I can hardly find them they are so small". Now thinking about it, I had been taking the Tumeric! Could they have been working! It isn't till now that I realize It could have been!

My kids were in the waiting room all day.

The head nurse came to see me in the recovery room, she was the most wonderful nurse, having no money for the hospital, they treated me like a queen. I thanked her so much for just keeping my children Informed. I told her I wanted to take her dinner, when all is better. Her response was, "well, I want you to take your children too!" I said okay, then she said, "THEY ARE SO FUNNY, HAD EVERYONE IN THE WAITING ROOM WERE IN STICHES, ALL DAY LONG THEY WENT TO THE CAFTERIA SEVERAL TIMES EVERYONE WAS LAUGHING." I knew what she meant yes, they are so good to be around. Very funny All the time. I am proud of them.

When I recovered I was told I needed Radiation. I did not want and told them let me think about it. I went home and took care of myself. I did not know I was supposed to have someone take care of Me, the nurse called me she was shocked told me I needed someone there. Oh well.

Now, I needed to think of the radiation, so, every Sunday I attend this church, same time same seat For the last four years. St. Therese, I was just sitting there and asked God for a sign that I did not need The radiation. I had learned early in life that you can talk to him like I can talk to anyone. I was in Church and I asked him, I left the church, now the timing was, one week before Easter.

On Easter Sunday, got to the church sat down in my regular seat, and WOW!! OH WOW, On the church altar was I saw the Image of the Shroud of Turn, Jesus face when he was wrapped in The garment cloth. I just could not believe it I asked the lady next to me if she could see it and she said No. Then I thought well, it is just for me. An EASTER IMAGE, ON EASTER SUNDAY!! I knew it was my sign. When the woman could not see it then I thought, "It is just for me." But, know something amazing, It took him over 56 years to "SHOW ME HIS FACE"! I would ask Jesus when I was six years old every day, "Jesus show me your face" and now" IN HIS TIME." I truly needed it! I was so in awe telling Jesus Thank you! I knew I did not need the treatments.

Well, going back to the hospital, I had to tell no to the treatments. One doctor got me and she hollered At me and told me that the cancer was going to come back and it will burst and it will be smelly. I told them I would deal with it when it comes back, you just take it out again. They were upset with me. Well, now I would go to church, and just sit there praying loving the image in the church, it was a feeling like no other. I just love to sit there, very empty. I asked to find a job I had no money.

This was now in May. It was easy, just to ask. I saw this Health Corporation, and I left Resume there in 5 min I was called, scheduled the next day for an interview, I got the job! I was at church thanking him oh, this is so good. I started to work as a driver, taking underserved Seniors, to doctor's appointments. I liked it. Well, I was doing good, then Christmas came I had enough money for my rent, and things that I needed but, I needed money for presents, I always Bought presents for my children and grandchildren. So, I am in church on the Weekdays, all the time I love it so, I told God. "Please give me some extra money Father, "JUST FOR CHRISTMAS PLEASE, JUST FOR CHRISTMAS". I went home I lived alone, and my son happened to be waiting, he said "Mom How are you?" I said "fine" He replied "Where were you?" I said "oh, I was at church.

My son came up to me got my hand and said "MOM THIS IS JUST FOR CHRISTMAS". JUST FOR CHRISTMAS". He had my hand and gave me $500.00. I was so stunned, "GOD ANSWERS!" JUST ASK! NO COINCIDENCE.

So, A new year 2008, in fact FEBRUARY, almost Easter. I developed a nodule on my Thyroid, it was big. Where I worked for the SENIOR CENTER, we had doctors on the facility, I showed them and they told me go and get MRI right away. I went to the doctor and they gave me the examination and said yes, that is A tumor on your Thyroid, a biopsy was scheduled.

I went to church. I sat there, I told him, God I don't care if it is a nodule just do not let it be cancer. Next morning, 5 in the morning, I was in the room with the doctor, I could see the big white lights in the Room and the picture of the tumor of my thyroid. The doctor said this will not take long, and he had the long needle in his hand, well he has this little machine going round, and round on my neck, and then he shuts the lights off and said "YOU HAVE NOTHING!" I got up and said "YES! I KNOW WHAT IT IS!!, AND I LEFT. THANK YOU, MY FATHER!

During the week, I would pick up my grandson from school and take him home. On this day, I told him I want to stop at church, and pray, then I take you home. He said, "Okay grandma". I was sitting In church he sat in back of me and started yelling "GRANDMA! WHY IS JESUS COMING BACK?" I said You see it? He said Yes, Then I knew others can see it! How wonderful, How very wonderful, I told him not to be afraid but to pray for what he needs. Yes!

I started to tell people, I would take them and share, some would never talk to me again. I do not know why. I did show priests, one ran out, another one asked me to write his name down and ask that I pray for him. One visiting priest started to cry, he said that His father had died, and he was not able to attend his funeral but seeing this he knew his father was all right!

There was a man, who my brother asked me to meet him in the church, with his wife, we met an I asked Him if he believed in THE SHROUD OF TURIN, he said he truly did, he did not finish sitting down and was So amazed at what he saw told me to look at the hairs on his arm standing up he asked how long it was there, I told him, he then told me, "MARILYN, I HAVE STAGE 4 LIVER CANCER, THEY GIVE ME TWO MONTHS TO LIVE. I TOLD HIM, THEN PRAY FOR WHAT YOU NEED. About 9 mos later, I saw him coming out with his BOY'S CLUB, they had come back from a trip. He saw me and he was happy.

He said, "THERE IS MY ANGEL," I told him "IT IS YOUR FAITH, HE LIVED 2 ½ more years. Died at 81. I loved just going to sit at the church, very empty during the week. When it was dark and gloomy outside The image would be like a neon sign, SOOOOOO clear.

EASTER 2013, I got this growth on my neck, clavicle area, I felt it growing and you know it did not Bother me nor did I think anything, well, it started to get big. I was not working anymore, I went to this Free Clinic. The doctor saw it and he had consultation with other doctors, they were going to take it out. I agreed and then, they sent it for biopsy, I was called back 2 days later. The doctor told me that my Cancer had come back, and it has probably spread, will go to my lungs or to my brain. I told him, I do not feel any tumors, where are they?

He said in the breast. I thought he was crazy. So, I left. I did not do anything till I started to feel the Tumors in my breast, growing. Yes, GROWING.

I went to the hospital, different one, they did me 5 biopsies. NOW THIS IS BACK TO CHAPTER ONE, "I AM NOW DYING". 'YOU HAVE A FEW MONTHS TO LIVE. YOU NEED CHEMO AND RADIATION. YES HOW DO I TELL MY KIDS We left the hospital in shock, talking very little, we were both in shock.

Trying to understand what is happening. I went to get a body scan, and this is a different doctor, a second opinion. He says "Yes" you need the treatment 8 tumors, five in one breast, 2 in the other and one in the Lymphnode. I went home told my children I needed a meeting with them, they came over very quickly. I told them What the doctors had found, everyone just sitting there in silence, I also told them I was not going for The treatments, they were stunned, I told them why, I was not going to die from "CANCER" just The complications, from the treatments. I know they were disappointed, but one thing, my children have always respected, my wishes. My one son took me to get a third opinion, well, the doctor told him in front of me, "YOUR MOTHER IS IN DENIAL" Saddened, I was dying, that was that! "I WAS DYING." The ages of children, are 44,41,38 yrs, old, not "CHILDREN" but my grown "CHILDREN",I see the disappointment life has now changed I was trying to get this thru my head, I just was like, "WOW! Me this is Me." What is happening!

I started to think of the Church and the sign given to me back in 2006, and I thought I am going to" NEGOTIATE". I went to church empty, as usual, but I needed this with him.

Started to tell GOD, The image was so strong, 'OKAY YOU'RE THE ONLY ONE WHO CAN TELL ME WHEN I AM GOING TO DIE."

I AM NOT GOING TO WORRY ABOUT THIS ANYMORE. I AM JUST GOING TO DRINK BEER AND HAVE FUN WITH MY CHILDREN. FATHER THIS CANCER IS YOURS, YOU HANDLE IT.

BUT WHEN YOU GET READY TO TAKE ME, JUST GIVE ME 2 WEEKS NOTICE TO GET MY PAPER WORK IN ORDER, NO PAIN AND I WILL

GLADY GO WITH YOU, BUT FATHER I JUST NEED ANOTHER SIGN.

There was this janitor who I always saw cleaning the church. Very hard working. I saw him many times I did not know him, so I called to him, I introduced my self to him and I asked him if he believed in the SHROUD OF TURIN? He said YES! I believe. I told him I wanted to show him something, and he came over to where I was sitting, he sat down and, just started to cry, thought it was beautiful, wanted to know the history, I did tell him and he was in awe. He then told me that He travels thru bike and bus, 5 cities to get to this job and then he said the most wonderful thing," I WILL NEVER BE SICK, NOW THAT I KNOW THIS IS HERE! I WILL SEE IT EVERYDAY." MARIANO, SUCH A GREAT HEART.

So, he told me I have something I want you to have, I would have given it to my mother, but she has to many things on her alter at home, I then thought my girlfriend, but no, you need this. This is for you. He left and came back, this is from ITALY, written in Italian, he gave it to me. OH MY GOD! I look at it, I took it, and put it to my heart. I knew GOD was answering, IT WAS THE FACE IMPRINT A COPY OF THE SHROUD OF TURIN. I SAID TO GOD" GOD, I KNOW WHAT YOU ARE SAYING, "MARILYN HOW MANY TIMES TO I NEED TO GIVE YOU MY FACE?

I got up and left happy and just so at peace and without a care in world. NO TREATMENTS! Well as time went

25

on, I started to feel the tumors, at night and I began to understand the Bible, the Part where Jesus is on the cross suffering, and he prays to his father and asked "FATHER, WHY HAVE YOU FORSAKEN ME. Jesus was human and had pain. I get it, I truly get it. I opened a book by DR. JOSEPH MURPHY, I asked God to give me an answer, about all of this, HONEST! INDIAN, I opened it And at the top of the page it said "JESUS SAID THY FAITH HAS HEALED THEE" Oh golly he is with and Walking with me this whole time. AMAZING! remember when I was 6 yrs. old, I would ask him to show me his face in my hands, He took 56 years to show me his face,"" IN HIS TIME.

It was the time I needed, me always praying when I was young, and he shows me I get it, I TRULY NEEDED IT AT THIS TIME.

We all decided that I move in with my son. I sold everything. I started living With my son. He would go across the border, and he knew this girl who ran a deli. They had a fruit that they said was good for cancer. But was not allowed here, so they cleaned it, froze it, and they brought it to me. I remembered I was in Colorado and saw a tree, called the BRAZILIAN PAW PAW, it stated it was a cancer cure, I Googled it and found the supplement store in OKLAHOMA, it was GUANABANA, from that fruit my son brought me, but it was also called GRAVIOLA! I called the store and asked about the supplements, he asked me "YOU HAVE CANCER"? I said yes, they are giving me a few months to live. He told me take 6 a day. $15.00 dollars a bottle. Okay, I will do that. I started to take it, and I was okay with it, I still made my visits, with doctors, still insisting that I Get the chemo and radiation, yes, they were very upset, so I asked why can't you just remove the Breasts, they stated I was too far gone.

Okay for six weeks I was taking GRAVIOLA, I started to feel the tumors getting small, and I would laugh, YES! I WAS LAUGHING. Six weeks go by I go to see the Doctor's And, they gave an Xray, the one doctor comes out running and said I have nothing!! Yes, no tumors.

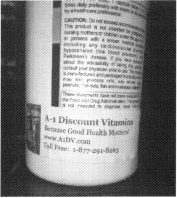

The doctor told me you have nothing my son was with me. They stood staring at me I told them what I had taken. Not even the one in the lymnode, they were stunned. I had nothing!! But I will always be stage 4!

I told them what I took, I called the vitamin place, I told them what happened, they said, it takes away

PANCREATIC, STOMACH, LIVER, COLON PROSTRATE, BREAST TUMORS, BUT THE FDA WILL NOT APPROVE IT. No one could tell me where the tumors went.

I have talked to people about this Graviola, today but doctors scare you with the word "CANCER". With the little time I had left I would have been in bed, suffering from the after effects that the Chemo and radiation will present, and be in bed and what! Die a few months later, no, God gave Me a sign, and I believe him. I will not die of Cancer, I will die from all the complications that the The treatments will do to me.

Now no tumors? Where have they gone, the doctors, just do not know what to do.

So, with that I was happy, wow oh wow, God hears, how can he not, The Bible states (ALL CURES ARE FOUND ON EARTH). My sign was in the church, Yes, he hears. The only thing I was so dumb after awhile I stopped Taking the Graviola, (I WAS SO DUMB).

2016 comes, I was still seeing the doctors, and they still insisted that I needed the treatments. Well sure enough there was a growth on my right breast, but it was growing fast. So, doctors are telling me that they need to remove my right breast, I said but you told me back in 2013, when I asked to just removed the breasts, you said that I was too far gone that my cancer had spread. I started with the Graviola again and made the arrangements to have the Tumor removed. I did not have a biopsy done.

Now getting ready for the surgery, it was to be done in June, early first week. The doctors Explaining what they were going to do and how the operation was going to happen, Also I need the chemo and radiation, I said no, I did not want. Well, the one surgical doctor stepped Out of my procedure and refused, because she stated that I did not believe in "MEDICAL SCIENCE" I told them that I honor their medical field and how they have dedicated themselves to becoming What they are but it was not for me. She still refused, Yes, they were upset.

I was worried, I could not understand, but I believed in God, I knew he gave me the sign.

I would go and sit there in the church I would just love it. It is very relaxing.

On April 29th, I always wish my Grandfather, HAPPY BIRTHDAY, It has been 47 years that he has been gone. My grandfather, who was so into religion, OUR LADY OF LOURDES, I told him, "Grandpa I wish I had the money to go to Lourdes, France to the Healing waters, just like you and my grandmother did, But have a great birthday.

A week later was my birthday, and I get a FED EX PACKAGE IN THE MAIL, I opened and, I was just in A standstill speechless way, it was a BOTTLE OF WATER FROM LOURDES. My cousin Jimmy sent it from Lourdes, France, with a note telling me he was at the healing waters, and he was filling the bottle of water himself, he stated that he had it with him when he was on his bike, riding thru the Payrenes Mountains, and felt that is what kept him safe, and he was he was now sending the water to me, half way around the world, because he knew I would love it! HE DID NOT KNOW I WAS GOING IN FOR SURGERY! I was thanking God, so much. NO COINCIDENCE.

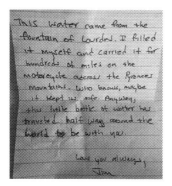 

A couple of nights passed and I heard the phone ring around 3:00 am. I answered but no one was there. I just put the phone down, and started to drift off to sleep, I

Clearly heard a voice tell me "YOUR FAITH HAS HEALED THEE". I opened my eyes, and I just Thanked God, because, it is said that during those hours of the morning, it is the best time to Talk with him, I had heard that a long time ago.

I had a dream 2 weeks before I went in for surgery, I was sitting in the church that I go to.

I love it. In the dream the church turned in to this beautiful temple, so big, and just so wonderful. A door opened, a little girl came out, she said "Hi Marilyn" I just looked at her, and she looked like my cousin, that had died when she was 3 yrs, and I was 6yrs, old, I had not thought of her

In years, I said "BARBARA, it is so good to see you, she told me, "MARILYN WOULD YOU LIKE TO SEE GOD?" I said" Yes" then she said, COME OVER HERE, I WENT INTO THIS BEAUTIFUL ROOM, LIT SO BRIGHT, YET SO TRANQUIL, she closed the door, I just loved the feeling, I was like floating just my Head, could not see my body, I was saying "OH I COULD LIVE HERE FOREVER, I LOVE IT HERE.

Then there was this beautiful sky blue lite in front of me, it started to embrace my body, I could see the Light coming from his hands, on my arms on my back to his chest, one hand was under my head and the other hand embraced me to God. I felt so amazing and God was embracing me like I was a child, and it was "SUCH A WONDERFUL, GLORIOUS FEELING." I have never experienced before. I did not want it to end I Loved it. I THEN SAID "GOD IS" and I woke up. I was told that was the way Solomon was embraced by God, it is stated in the Bible, I was surprised, I never read the Bible, to that extent.

My dream of God, I will never forget. I was his child I saw that I cannot explain the wonderful love I was feeling, something I have never experienced in my whole life.

So, now my surgery was scheduled, and was going to be 9 hours, they were going to remove the the growth and going to remove the whole right breast. I did get my bottle of Lourdes water and I put on the breast, I told God to let happen what he wants to happen. My children were crying as I was being rolled to the surgery room. My children were crying, so sad to see, but "LOVE" FILLED THE ROOM. I gave my life to God, and I knew he was with me. Yes, the staff is still going on, about how I need the CHEMO AND RADIATION, but no that wasn't to be argued, my mind was made up.

So, my surgery was completed, I had been cut from the top of my back all the way down to my waist, Up and around the right front breast, they needed the back skin to cover the breast. Staples all the way down my back. The first week staples were popping out and I needed a caregiver. It was ugly. This was a a new procedure, the doctor brought other doctors to see it. I showed my kids with the staples open and stuff oozing out I told them "I AM NOT GOING TO DIE OF CANCER, BUT OF THIS MESS!

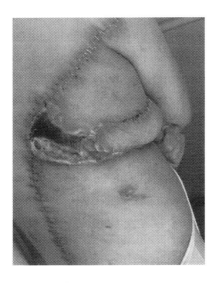

So, the pathology report comes out, BENIGN, BENIGN, BENIGN, ONLY THE TUMOR HAD CANCER.

BUT YOU STILL NEED CHEMO AND RADIATION. Does not make sense, my body was filled with cancer.

Metastatic breast Cancer that is what I was told, I had. ONLY THE TUMOR HAD CANCER!

For four months, I had this ugly ozzing hole in my back, the caregiver would come to my house and Change the tape, it was a mess, I hated it and doctors still saying you need Chemo, You need Radiation. My dog, MEXICO would walk the caregiver in and when finished walked him out. She was so Attentive to me, she was a CHIHUAHUA, 11yrs old. She slept with me stayed by my side. She did not like JACK N the BOX burgers, she like McDonalds, so, human like, I would put makeup On her and she would be watching, I would ask her you want makeup? I would act like I put Her eyebrow pencil and then lipstick, I would tell her, "your pretty" and she would strut away. At the end of October I was finally healed, from my back, and the caregiver, was so happy and very Nice.

The next week I awoke to find Mexico panting, and next to me, my bed was full of blood, I got dressed and hurried to the Dog Hospital, she still had blood coming out, the doctor examined her And he was so stressed, he then told me, "MARILYN I CHECKED HER TWO WEEKS AGO GAVE HER SHOTS, SHE WAS FINE"! "SHE HAS TUMORS COMING OUT OF HER! WE HAVE TO PUT HER DOWN. I stayed with her till she passed, telling her how much I loved her and how she was a wonderful Dog. Then she passed. I was in mourning for a long time, I truly missed her, but like I said GOD, has his way of coming and clearing things up.

I went to see a movie "A DOG'S PURPOSE", I sat threw it and I knew why my Mexico died. Wonderful movie to see. SHE TOOK MY TUMORS I truly believe that. I thanked God, Because I understood. See the movie "A DOG'S PURPOSE", you will understand. I had a dog before Mexico, her name was KITTY, she was tiny, white, and she loved Pizza, Kitty, also watch me put make up on, comb my hair for work, and I would put make up on her And she would just strut away happy. I had a gallbladder surgery, and I took long to get well, so Kitty was always by my side, and just watching me. I petted her head and told her to go to sleep, I wasn't feeling good. I had a dream of my mother, standing at my bed and she told me, "MARILYN, I AM GOING TO TAKE KITTY". I said okay, she pick her up and flew in the sky away. I woke up and I called my son, I told him that, Grammie came to take KITTY, in my dream, and she did. I told my son just check her, she was at the foot of my bed. He then went to touch her and she was gone. I was not feeling good like floating in the air, and so I went to sleep my son buried her. On the next day, I dreamt of Kitty and I said "OH, KITTY YOU'RE HERE, YOU'RE HERE, I WAS TOUCHING HER HEAD, AND ALL OF A SUDDEN I felt this wet hand, I woke up and my hand was BLOODY, I went to emergency and I was Hemorrhaging KITTY, saved my life. I missed her too. So when I saw a DOG's PURPOSE, this movie explained a lot to me. SEE THE MOVIE!

Answers are all around us, we just need to look.

Going back for the checkup, the breast surgeon told me I still needed CHEMO, and this is what he said, "Rosalie, if you were a 80 yrs old woman sickly with a walker, I would not have you put that poison in Your system!! I said, Right POISON! He replied," I did not say that". I told him that is what came out of his mouth. I said "THANK YOU GOD" A month later they I go for A MRI SCAN, They found a tumor in the lymphnode, I saw it. So first thing you need Chemo, I said "no, set me up for a biopsy, well, they did not wait they said "LET US DO IT NOW! The workers, feeling so sorry for me, they know my history, I said to them, 'WHEN THEY FIND NOTHING, CALL ME I WILL TELL YOU MY SECRET! Within 2 days later I make the visit to see the CANCER DOCTOR, she looked at me and said "YOU HAVE NOTHING" she stands there staring at me.

Yes, a week later that worker called me and wanted the "Secret" I gave it to her. In her hand. So, now the Cancer Center, the cancer doctor, told me. "MARILYN, YOU ARE DISEASED FREE! YOU HAVE NOTHING! WHERE DID THE TUMORS GO.?

So, I want to share this, I want to share all of it, I believe. I trusted. The world is open to all of us to see the beauty and tools that are available to us to use. There are wonderful books out there that talk about this and how we create and can fix our lives and illnesses, take the time to study and get to see how the world was created with all this help. GOD CREATED A BEAUTIFUL WORLD, TAKE

THE TIME TO SEE AND APPRECIATE. Life is beautiful, it is the situations we create that spoil it.

I feel we know our own body, truly know it. I believe in God. I believe in after life awareness, Our grandparents, parents, all of have passed, that is "LOVE" they are love and love does not die! They are always around in spirit, these are our ANCESTORS, believe. Always just say hello! If I had gone with the treatments, I would of shown no faith, GOD TRULY ANSWERED ME. 56 years to show me his face, when I needed it truly needed it I was 6 yrs old when I asked him to let me see his face, IN HIS TIME, It is hard being diagnosed with CANCER, it scares you.

It was how I felt. BUT IT IS SO TRUE! JUST GIVE IT TO HIM HE WILL SHOW YOU THE WAY!

We are adults, and we forget how to pray, He is our father we are still his children. When we were young and innocent, we would bring papers from school, to be signed by our parents, for Permission to go on a field trip or, sign our report cards, we gave it to our parents, and they would Say "okay,"" You will have it by tomorrow. We went to bed, we did not get up 30 times a night to see if it was signed, WHY? Because we trusted and we had faith in our parents. But as adults we get into the World of Money, Clothes, Jobs Family, and we "FORGET HOW TO PRAY"! HE IS THE ONLY ONE WE CAN ASK AND KNOW JUST KNOW HE WILL GIVE IT TO YOU.

WE ARE GOD'S CHILDREN, JUST KNOW HE
HEARS, HE HAS A PLAN, YES, IT IS HARD, I
KNOW THIS I TRULY DO. IT WAS HARD FOR
ME, I WAS DYING! I AM ASKING YOU TO JUST
TRUST. GIVE HIM YOUR PROBLEMS,

* BECAUSE*

"GOD IS"

For Graviola supplements: <u>WWW.A1DV.COM</u> 877 291
8263, Turmeric Curcumin Supplements,

TUMERIC CURCUMIN SUPPLEMENTS

VITAMIN B17

THIS I *SWEAR* IS TRUE

ABOUT THE AUTHOR

BORN May 8, 19 old, and she can probably be your grandmother.

She is not a" CEO" of any company, nor a" Movie Star," a" Model," or a" Singer" like all

These wonderful singers out today. She feels that she is just an "ORDINARY JOE".

Just wanted to share a session of her life that over the years, now being a senior, we should take a step back a take a look at our lives starting from childhood, how many wonderful, mystical things

Come into our life that we just pass it by and claim it is our imagination.

My children are my best friends and have encouraged me to write this, so that it will help many people.

You will truly understand when you have read "THIS I SWEAR IS TRUE", because it is.

BRIEF DISCRIPTION

I invite you to read this book once, then again, and again. You will have a hard time believing, yes, it is all

Truth. Any fatal illness is so hard, to believe, especially the one with the "C" word. This is very scary

For anyone, you want something done right now and you become a terrible wreck, we do not think.

"THIS IS NOT HAPPENING"," HOW CAN THIS BE", of course it is hard to handle.

Reading, this will really change you, because I am not anyone special, but I truly believed. You will

Learn how to change anything with the POWER OF GOD WITHIN.

So, after reading, please SHARE, SHARE SHARE.

I will close for now we can change our lives for the better. Get to know your body, and get to know GOD. Please believe what I have written, because "THIS I SWEAR IS TRUE"

Printed in the United States
By Bookmasters